A little something
for your bundle
on the way...
Congrats! Love,
The Hachman
Ones ♡

For sweet baby

_____

From

<u>Charlotte + Cecilia Hachmaw</u>

On this day

<u>March 19, 2006</u>

Birthdate

Weight

Length

Sugar & Spice

Illustrated by Becky Kelly

Written by Patrick Regan

Andrews McMeel Publishing

Kansas City

For information write Andrews McMeel Publishing,

4520 Main Street, Kansas City, Missouri 64111.

www.beckykelly.com

03 04 05 06 07 EPB 10 9 8 7 6 5 4 3 2 1

ISBN: 0-7407-3911-5

Illustrations by Becky Kelly

Design by Stephanie R. Farley

Edited by Polly Blair

Production by Elizabeth Nuelle

for little
rebecca-
who captures
my heart.
bk

Sugar & Spice

When a new baby girl
Comes into the world,
The angels rejoice up above.

The moon and stars beam . . .

As a child is received
Into hearts that await with pure love.

So freshly arrived . . .
So perfectly formed . . .

Silken cheeks painted with rose . . .

A bundle of joy . . .

From the top of her head,

Right down
        to her sweet
little toes.

From sugar and spice
And everything nice
They say little girls can be made . . .

But it took more than this
To create the small miss . . .

Who's just joined
life's joyous parade.

A sprinkle of sunshine
Has brightened her smile,

And added a spark to her eyes . . . .

A whisper of whimsy
And wee bit of wonder
Like yeast, help her spirits to rise.

A cupful of giggles . . .

And spoonful of dreams
Will give life the flavor of fun . . .

Add a dash of panache
And a dollop of daring
For adventurous goals to be won.

To all the above
Add unlimited love
And mix with the greatest of care . . .

You'll have one little girl,
As sweet as can be . . .

The answer to life's fondest prayer.